SPIRITU

HEALING THROUGH THE SACRAMENTS

———❦———

by
Fr Jim McManus C.Ss.R.

*All booklets are published thanks to the
generous support of the members of the
Catholic Truth Society*

CATHOLIC TRUTH SOCIETY

PUBLISHERS TO THE HOLY SEE

To love and be loved is, therefore, the ultimate goal of every human action, the deepest desire of every human heart. Sadly, at times, we can be very misguided in our search for love. We can choose ways of living or acting which are totally opposed to true love. We can settle for pseudo love. Instead of bringing peace and joy, pseudo love wounds the heart. It prevents the person from discovering his or her true self. As the Second Vatican Council said:

> If human beings are the only creatures on earth that God has wanted for their own sake, they can fully discover their true selves only in sincere self-giving.[3]

Discovering our true selves

Notice the true path of self-discovery: self-giving, not self-seeking. St John Paul II developed this insight of the Second Vatican Council and defined our capacity to love in this way:

> We have the power to express love – precisely that love in which the human person becomes a gift and thorough this gift fulfils the meaning of his or her being and existence.[4]

Loving as God loves involves making that sincere gift of self. If it is not self-giving it is not love. Notice the big bonus for making this gift of self: we discover our true selves,

---

[3] Second Vatican Council, *Gaudium et Spes: Pastoral Constitution on the Church in the Modern World*, 24.

[4] St John Paul II, *Theology of the Body* (Pauline Press, Boston, 2006) 15:1.

we become happy. As St John Paul II said so succinctly, "happiness means being rooted in love".[5] Everyone wants to be happy but not everyone wants to love in a self-giving way and so they do not achieve happiness.

The price of happiness, then, is sincere self-giving. Sadly, because of our sinful weakness, we are not always willing to pay that price. We seek happiness in self-seeking, in selfishness, in self-centeredness, in speaking or acting in ways that are contrary to true love. We can refuse to act in the likeness of God. We call that way of acting sin, which is always a failure to love.

In the *Catechism of the Catholic Church* (1992)[6] we have this very helpful definition of what we mean by sin:

> Sin is an offence against reason, truth and right conscience; it is failure in genuine love for God and neighbour caused by a perverse attachment to certain goods. It wounds the nature of man and injures human solidarity. It has been defined as "an utterance, a deed or a desire contrary to the eternal law".[7]

When I learnt my catechism a long time ago, I learnt off by heart this line: "*Sin is an offence against almighty God*". Today, however, the *Catechism* tells us that sin is an offence

---

[5] St John Paul II, *Theology of the Body* (Pauline Press, Boston, 2006) 16:2.

[6] This Catechism was promulgated by Pope St John Paul II on 11th October 1992, the 30th anniversary of the opening of the Second Vatican Council.

[7] *Catechism of the Catholic Church*, para 1849.

against "reason, truth and right conscience". If we believe that we have been made in the image and likeness of God, with the capacity to love as God loves, it is quite irrational to live in the hope of achieving happiness by acting against our human dignity as sons and daughters of God. Sin is an offence against God because it hurts and wounds the sons and daughters of God.

The sins of others against us and our own sins wound our very nature as human beings. This wound can then undermine and at times almost paralyse our power to express true love in sincere self-giving. Sin and the wound of sin can thus prevent us from discovering our true selves. That is why many people deep down can feel very unhappy and unfulfilled. They have never yet discovered their true selves through sincere self-giving.

Our surname is God

Jesus came to save us from our sins, to save us from the consequences of acting and living in a way that denies our deepest identity and dignity as sons and daughters of God our Father. Pope Francis expressed this very simply when he said:

> Are we aware of this gift? We are all God's children. Do we remember that in Baptism we received the seal of the heavenly Father and became his children? To say it simply: we bear God's surname. Our surname is God. He is the root of our vocation to holiness.[8]

---

[8] Pope Francis, Angelus on 1st November 2015.

We take our human father's surname as our own. As Christians, we also take our heavenly Father's surname. By becoming a human being, God the Son, as the Second Vatican Council said, "united himself in a certain way with each individual".[9] Jesus Christ became a brother to every single human being in history. Through his union with us we become sons and daughters of God his Father.

Healing the wound of sin

Jesus gave us three great sacraments for the healing of the wounds that the sins of others against us, and our own sins, inflict on our hearts: the Sacraments of Reconciliation, Anointing of the Sick and the Holy Eucharist. These sacraments are "the medicine of mercy" which we all need, saints and sinners alike, to live up to our true dignity as God's sons and daughters and to bear with pride our spiritual surname, which is God.

St Peter focuses our attention on the healing love and mercy of Christ with these words: "by his wounds we have been healed" (*1 P* 2:24) Every time we celebrate a sacrament we can say "by his wounds we are healed". Jesus gave us the sacraments so that his healing love can heal our wounds, restore our trust and re-energise us in living our Christian lives.

---

[9] *Gaudium et Spes*, 22.

Our inner wounds

We know from our own experience that we can be easily hurt by the words, attitudes and actions of others. When we say we have been hurt we really mean that a wound has been inflicted on our hearts, in our innermost being, where our capacity to love exists. As a result we might find it very hard to love the person who has hurt us. We might even try to justify not loving that person on the grounds that they deliberately tried to hurt us. Instead of loving we can harden our hearts. While it is painful enough to be hurt, it is spiritually more painful to harden one's heart because, in the refusal to make the sincere gift of self, even to the enemy, we rob ourselves of the opportunity of discovering our true selves. Then we have to live with our false self, the self that God didn't create. We can begin to settle for hardness of heart, and allow resentments and even bitterness to rob us of inner peace and serenity. If we remain in this hardness we can never really discover our true selves and we condemn ourselves to live sad lives, locked inside our hearts, expecting everyone to love us without ever returning that love. It is then that we really need to experience the healing power of the sacraments.

The Church as a field hospital

Pope Francis spelt out very clearly his vision of the healing ministry of the Church when he said:

I see clearly that the thing the Church needs most today is the ability to heal wounds and to warm the hearts of the faithful; it needs nearness, proximity. I see the Church as a field hospital after battle. It is useless to ask a seriously injured person if he has high cholesterol and about the level of his blood sugars! You have to heal his wounds. Then we can talk about everything else. Heal the wounds, heal the wounds… And you have to start from the ground up.[10]

Because our hearts were created by God to love, sin, which is a refusal to love, devastates the heart and robs it of true inner peace and joy. The heart that refuses to love is a sick heart in great need of healing. Physically the person with this sick heart may look strong and fit and in control, but on the inside they are in an inner turmoil, bereft of true peace. Love alone fulfils the heart.

Christ's parable of the prodigal son encourages us never to lose heart. No sin, no matter how great, is unforgiveable. God forgives all our sins the moment we turn to him and ask for forgiveness. As Pope Francis repeats so often, "God never tires of forgiving us, we too often tire of asking for forgiveness". God heals the broken heart; he restores supernatural life to the soul who rejected it; he fills the heart with the Holy Spirit. When we turn to Jesus in love, asking for his mercy, he assures us with these words, "If anyone loves me he will keep my word, and my Father will

---

[10] Interview in *America Magazine*, 30th September 2013.

love him and we shall come to him and make our home with him" (*Jn* 14:23). That is the transforming miracle of the sacraments. Every time we celebrate the sacraments, God the Father, with his Son Jesus Christ, makes his home in our heart. Our inner being, our heart, becomes heaven on earth. God is dwelling within us. Through the faithful celebration of the sacraments the sinful heart becomes a heaven where God loves to dwell.

In this booklet we will reflect on the transforming miracle of Confession, when God forgives all our sins, heals the wounds inflicted on our hearts by sin, and purifies and restores our capacity to love as Christ loves. We will also discuss the healing gift of the sacrament of the Anointing of the Sick, in which Jesus comes to fill the sick person with his healing love and peace. And, keeping the good wine to last, we will reflect on how, in the great sacrament of the Holy Eucharist, we can offer to God all our joys and sorrows, all our successes and failures, all our sins and all our virtues, and how God receives all and transforms all. The Holy Eucharist is the greatest of all the sacraments, the ultimate source of healing.

HEALING WOUNDED LOVE IN THE SACRAMENT OF CONFESSION

God created us to love. He endowed us with the capacity to love with our whole heart and to find our human fulfilment in that love. But, through our own sins and the sins of others against us, our hearts can be wounded; our very capacity to love can be almost paralysed. Christ wants to forgive us our sins, but he also wants to heal the wounds that sin, our own and others' against us, has inflicted on us. As St Peter said, "by his wounds we have been healed" (*1 P* 2:24).

We have always believed that in the sacrament of Confession all our sins are forgiven, but we have not very often reflected on how the wounds that sin inflicts on our hearts are also healed. That is why Blessed Pope Paul VI, when he promulgated the new Rite of Penance,[11] called the sacrament "a sacrament of healing". He wrote:

> In order that this sacrament of healing may truly achieve its purpose among Christ's faithful, it must take root in their whole lives and lead them to more fervent service of God and neighbour.

He identified what is healed in the sacrament in this way:

> Just as the wound of sin is varied and multiple in the life of individuals and of a community, so the healing which penance provides is varied.[12]

There is a multiple wound of sin which can undermine and even poison our relationship with others. Indeed the wounds of sin can distort relationships within a whole community or society. Sectarian hatred is one example of how the wounds of sins, so often ancestral sins, can continue to polarise communities around the world long after the original wounds were inflicted.

The firm belief that all our sins are forgiven in the sacrament of Confession has been a source of great peace and joy for Catholics, freeing us from the burden of guilt. But we haven't paid sufficient attention to the sacrament's power to heal the inner wounds inflicted by sin. Before we

---

[11] The popular title for this sacrament is Confession. That is what we do. We confess our sins. But it is also called, in the official document of the Church, the sacrament of Penance or the sacrament of Reconciliation.

[12] Blessed Paul VI, *New Rite of Penance*, 7.

reflect on this healing dimension of the sacrament it will be profitable to briefly reflect on sin and the conditions necessary for committing sin.

The conditions for sin

The Church has very clear teaching on the interior conditions which must be present to commit a serious sin. We must be fully free to make the decision to act in a sinful way; we must also have full knowledge that what we are planning to do is against the whispering of our conscience; and we must give our full consent to the decision knowing that it is wrong. In other words, we have to have our wits about us to commit a serious sin. We have to be fully conscious of what we are doing.

Conscience

Our conscience is our guide. The Second Vatican Council gave us this very clear definition of what our conscience is and how it guides us:

> Deep within their consciences men and women discover a law which they have not laid upon themselves and which they must obey. Its voice, ever calling them to love and do what is good and to avoid evil, tells them inwardly at the right moment: do this, shun that. For they have in their hearts a law inscribed by God. Their dignity rests in observing this law, and by it they will be judged. Their conscience is people's most secret core, and their sanctuary. There they are alone with God,

whose voice echoes in their depths. By conscience, in a most wonderful way, that law is made known that is fulfilled in love of God and love of one's neighbour.[13]

Our conscience in which "the voice of God echoes" protects our vocation in life, which is to love, and shows us the way we should walk. St John Paul II summed up the vocation of each person with these words: "Love is the fundamental and innate vocation of every human being".[14] Our conscience keeps watch over our vocation to love. It will immediately alert us if we are in danger of violating our love in any way. If we violate our vocation to love, by self-seeking, refusing to be self-giving, we not only rob ourselves of the opportunity of discovering our true selves, as we saw in the previous chapter, but we also feel guilty. We have inflicted a wound on our inner being. As the *Catechism of the Catholic Church* says, "Sin wounds the nature of man and injures human solidarity."[15] If the violation of love is grave, the guilt will also be grave. Then the person experiences "a guilty conscience" which robs him or her of inner peace and serenity. The only way to be freed from that guilt is by acknowledging one's sin and asking God's forgiveness. God alone can absolve the conscience of guilt. Therapist Brennan Mullaney writes: "Absolution, authentic

---

[13] *Gaudium et Spes*, 16.

[14] St John Paul II, *The Role of the Christian Family in the Modern World*, 11.

[15] *Catechism of the Catholic Church*, para 1849.

resolution of severe guilt, without God is a therapeutic impossibility", and he goes on to say: "A therapist who does not believe in God, or one who feels unable to lead a guilty patient to God by spiritual counselling, is ethically bound to acknowledge that limitation and to refer the person for qualified spiritual guidance."[16]

Sacrament for the forgiveness of sin

The sacrament of Confession is the great gift that Christ gave to the Church for absolving sin, freeing the conscience of guilt, and restoring the loving relationship with God and neighbour. Jesus gave the Church that great sacrament, after his resurrection, when he appeared to the Apostles on that first Easter Sunday. He said to them:

> "Peace be with you. As the Father sent me so I am sending you." After saying this he breathed on them and said: "Receive the Holy Spirit. If you forgive anyone's sins, they are forgiven. If you retain anyone's sins they are retained" (*Jn* 20:20-23).

The Risen Lord, fully aware of our sinful, human weakness, gave to his Church, with those words "Receive the Holy Spirit", this wonderful sacrament through which all sins, even the greatest, are forgiven.

Only God can take away guilt and restore peace to the conscience once it has been lost through serious sin. The

---

[16] J. Brennan Mullaney, *Authentic Love: Theory and Therapy* (St Pauls, New York, 2008) p. 176.

Catholic who has forgotten about this great sacrament, or who has refused to humbly confess his or her serious sin to the priest, will try to find other ways of alleviating the guilty conscience. But as Mullaney says:

> The voice of conscience, love's protector, does not allow dilution, equivocation, political compromise or escape. Its indictments and verdicts are absolute because love is absolute. When we have transgressed the law of love, we know it – absolutely. For this reason, both psychologically and spiritually, guilt can be resolved, erased, only by *absolution*. [17]

Guilt, of course, is the appropriate response to any violation of love. It is the voice of the Holy Spirit whispering in the depths of conscience that a wound has been inflicted on the heart. It is the Spirit's way of appealing to the poor sinner to be reconciled with God.

Sacrament for the healing of the wound of sin

Carl Jung, one of the founding fathers of modern psychiatry and psychology, who wasn't a Catholic, had a very high regard for the sacrament of Confession. Seventy years ago, Jung was writing about how Catholics found in Confession a marvellous protection against all kinds of neurotic manifestations. He wrote:

---

[17] J. Brennan Mullaney, *Authentic Love: Theory and Therapy* (St Pauls, New York, 2008) p. 177.

The fact is there are relatively few neurotic Catholics, and yet they are living under the same conditions as we do. They are presumably suffering from the same social conditions and so on, and so one would expect a similar amount of neurosis. There must be something in the cult, in the actual religious practice, which explains that peculiar fact that there are fewer complexes, or that these complexes manifest themselves much less in Catholic than in other people. That something, besides confession, is really the cult itself. It is the Mass.[18]

Having researched this phenomenon about there being relatively few neurotic Catholics he wrote:

You find the least or the smallest number of complex manifestations in practising Catholics, far more in Protestants, and most in Jews... So there must be something in the Catholic Church which accounts for this peculiar fact. Of course, we think in the first place of Confession.[19]

The 'complex manifestations' that Jung speaks about are manifestations of buried guilt. Jung was very aware that the Catholic who goes to Confession comes away free of guilt. And, as the leading psychologist and therapist of his time, that fact intrigued him. Jung was not observing the sacramental forgiveness of sin, which brings the inner

---

[18] C. G. Jung, *The Collected Works* (Routledge, London, 1977) vol. 18, p. 613.

[19] C. G. Jung, *The Collected Works* (Routledge, London, 1977) vol. 18, p. 613.

peace. He was observing the fact that Catholics who go to Confession have a great way of coping with guilt, anxiety and fear. As he researched this phenomenon he discovered that:

> A large percentage, by far the majority of Catholics said that in the case of psychological trouble they would go to the priest and not the doctor. The vast majority of Protestants said they would go to the doctor.[20]

It has been observed today that the increase in the numbers of Catholics going for counselling is in inverse proportion to the decline in the numbers going to Confession. If, to use Jung's phrase, the "complex manifestations" are the result of guilt, counselling, which is a form of secular confession, will not bring peace to the conscience. As Mullaney, quoted above, said, "Absolution, authentic resolution of severe guilt, without God, is a therapeutic impossibility".

Failure to open oneself to God's healing grace and forgiveness in the sacrament of Confession would deprive the person of the inner healing that we so often need as we make our way through this life. We should never be ashamed of admitting that we have been wounded by sin, our own or others', just as a patient visiting the doctor is not ashamed to talk about his or her ailments.

For our sins we need forgiveness; for the wounds of sin we need healing. We receive both in a good confession.

---

[20] C. G. Jung, *The Collected Works* (Routledge, London, 1977) vol. 18, p. 610.

St John Paul II reminded us: "The forgiven penitent is reconciled with himself in his inmost being, where he regains his own true identity".[21] As we "regain our true identity" we rejoice in knowing that God is our loving Father, that we are his beloved sons and daughters, that we bear his name. As Pope Francis said so clearly, "Our surname is God".[22] That is our true identity. If we forget this amazing revelation of who we truly are in God's sight, we should not be surprised if we develop, to use Jung's phrase, "neurotic manifestations".

Sin and the wound of sin

There is a very big difference between sin and the wound of sin. Sin itself, as we discussed above, is acting with full freedom, full knowledge and full consent. It is a very deliberate, fully conscious action that is against one's conscience. The wound of sin, on the other hand, is manifested by the person's reaction. A wound has been inflicted on the heart by someone's sinful word or action and now the broken-hearted person is reacting in a bad way. While the reaction may be quite bad, with all the appearances of being gravely sinful, if it is lacking one of the interior conditions for sin, namely full freedom, full knowledge or full consent, it is not a serious sin. The person, now feeling very guilty of committing a serious sin,

---

[21] St John Paul II, *On Reconciliation and Penance*, 31 V.

[22] Pope Francis, Angelus on 1st November 2015.

because of the bad reaction, may go to Confession, confess the sin, but make no reference to the deep hurt that was the cause of the bad reaction. The priest will give the penitent absolution, but what the person needs, most of all, is the healing of the deep hurt, the wound of sin. The reaction is a symptom of the hurt and until the hurt is healed the reaction will continue to happen.

Consider this example. A mother has been deeply hurt by her son. He obtained a lot of money from her over the years, he fell out with her when she was unable to give him any more, and now he refuses to speak to her or to allow his children to see their grandmother. She is very angry, rages against him to other members of her family, and frequently goes to Confession and confesses engaging in uncharitable talk. The confessor will encourage her to do her best not to engage in uncharitable gossip, give her absolution and tell her to go in peace. But the deep wound in her heart, the cause of all her bad reactions, has not been mentioned. Until her broken heart is healed, she will not have peace and she will most likely continue to criticise her son. What she needs most of all is the healing of the wounds that her son's sins against her have inflicted on her heart.

The concept of the wound of sin will be new to most penitents, just as it is new to many priests. The penitent should be encouraged to spend more time with "*Why did I do that?*" and less time on "*How often did I do that?*" They should then confess the *why* before the *how often*. For instance, the mother in the example, instead of confessing how often she criticises her son should really confess why she criticises him. She could begin her confession in this way: *Father, my heart is broken because my son refuses to speak to me or to allow his children to see me. I am so angry. I am always criticising him. I need God's help.* That would be a very good and complete confession. She brings her broken heart to the Lord. The priest then, after he gives her absolution, should pray with her in simple words like, *Lord Jesus, you came to bind up the broken heart. Your sister has brought her broken heart to you in this great sacrament of healing. Lord, as you have taken away all her sins heal now every wound of sin. Take away this pain. Heal her broken heart. And bless and forgive her son who has so deeply hurt her.* Her mother's heart has been wounded. But, once she begins to experience the healing of her heart she will be able to pray for her son rather than indulge in the criticism that distresses her. She will be able to peacefully accept her son, the way he is, in the knowledge that only God can change him.

The work of the Holy Spirit

There are two essential elements in the celebration of the sacrament of Reconciliation. First of all, the penitent, moved by the grace of the Holy Spirit, confesses his or her sins. The priest then, in the name of Jesus, pronounces absolution. Take a moment to reflect on this great prayer of absolution:

God, the Father of mercies, through the death and resurrection of his Son has reconciled the world to himself and sent the Holy Spirit among us for the forgiveness of sins; through the ministry of the Church may God give you pardon and peace, and I absolve you from your sins in the name of the Father, and of the Son, and of the Holy Spirit.

This prayer makes it clear that the Father of mercies, God our Father, is the source of all forgiveness. In the sacrament we are filled afresh with the Holy Spirit. We invite God's Spirit into every area of our lives, and we let go of all our worries and anxieties. The *Catechism of the Catholic Church*, speaking of the work of the Spirit in our lives, says:

Healing the wounds of sin, the Holy Spirit renews us interiorly through a spiritual transformation. He enlightens and strengthens us to live as "children of the light" through all that is good and right and true.[23]

Throughout Scripture God assures us that he "loves us with an everlasting love" (*Jr* 31:3), with a love that never changes. It is with this everlasting love of God that we are embraced when we respond to the grace of the Holy Spirit and enter into the great mystery of Christ's presence in the sacrament of Confession. It is to Christ that we are confessing our sins. Speaking of the nature of Confession, St John Paul II said:

---

[23] *Catechism of the Catholic Church*, para 1695.

It is a liturgical act, solemn in its dramatic nature, yet humble and sober in the grandeur of its meaning. It is the act of the Prodigal Son who returns to the Father and is welcomed by him.[24]

Reconciled with God and with one another

When we turn to God for forgiveness of our sins in the sacrament of Confession we have to be willing to share the forgiveness we receive with those who have sinned against us. God's forgiveness is never just for ourselves. It is for the whole family of God, for all our brothers and sisters. When you receive God's forgiveness you have the grace to forgive everyone in your life. We acknowledge this grace to forgive others each time we say the Lord's Prayer. We say to God our Father, "Forgive us our trespasses as we forgive those who trespass against us".

What is forgiveness?

There are many misunderstandings of what forgiveness is and what it means to forgive from the heart.[25] I will mention just a few. Forgiveness is not condoning or excusing a wrong nor is it tolerating it. We love the sinner but condemn the sin. We refuse to judge the person who

---

24 St John Paul II, *On Reconciliation and Penance*, 31.

25 For a more detailed study of the healing power of forgiveness see Jim McManus C.Ss.R. and Dr Stephanie Thornton, *Finding Forgiveness: Personal and Spiritual Perspectives* (Redemptorist Publications, 2006).

sins against us. Jesus says very clearly, "Judge not and you will not be judged" (*Mt* 7:1). Those who have been deeply hurt are tempted to sit in judgement on the ones who have sinned against them. Then the inner wound in their heart can turn septic and they are really inflicting a deeper wound on themselves. That wound will be healed as we celebrate the sacrament of Confession if we open it up to the Lord. We receive the grace to do what Jesus asks us to do when he says, "I say to you, love your enemies and pray for those who persecute you" (*Mt* 7:44).

Jesus, of course, would only ask us to do what is best for our health and true happiness. We don't have to be experts on mental health to understand that allowing the heart to become a storehouse for bitterness, resentment and unforgiveness cannot be good for one's health and happiness.

Science rediscovers the healing power of forgiveness

Stanford University in California carried out detailed research on how forgiving improves health. They invited five women, three Protestant and two Catholic, who had suffered the loss of either a husband or son through the violence in Northern Ireland. When they arrived, broken-hearted, at Stanford, they had a medical check-up before they were invited to enter into a week of training on forgiving. At the end of the week's training they had another medical check-up. Six months later, back in

Belfast, they had another medical check-up. These are some of the findings:

- On the measure of how hurt the Irish women felt by their loss, on a scale of 1 to 10, they began the week with a score of 8.5.

- When they left at the end of the week, they registered their hurt a bit over 3.5. When the questionnaires were returned at the six-month follow-up, their hurt score still stood below 4.

- The women reduced stress by almost half from the beginning of the training to the follow-up six months later.

- The women experienced an increase of forgiveness by 40% towards those who had killed their loved ones.

- Given a list of 30 items indicating depression, the women checked an average of 17 at the beginning, an average of 7 at the end of the training, and 10 at the six-month follow-up.

- The women also showed that by the follow-up assessment they had become significantly more optimistic.[26]

There are no drugs on the market that can get rid of so much pain and depression.

[26] For full details of the Stanford research see Dr Fred Luskin, *Forgive For Good* (Harper, San Francisco, 2002).

Professor Robert Enright, by his pioneering research, has brought about a revolution in the study of forgiveness in the USA. He has provided very clear evidence that forgiving has direct effects in decreasing anxiety and depression and improving self-esteem. Indeed, it has been said that Enright's evidence shows that forgiveness may be "as important to the treatment of emotional and mental disorders as…sulfa drugs and penicillin have been to the treatment of infectious diseases."[27]

Jesus, knowing all our human weakness, asks us to forgive "seventy-seven times" (*Mt* 18:22). In other words, Jesus who came so that we may "have life and have it to the full" (*Jn* 10:10) gives us the secret of keeping our heart in peace and enjoying "life to the full", even when we find ourselves in difficult relationships. The secret is unconditional forgiveness to the best of our human limitations.

Only God can love and forgive unconditionally. Before the person with the broken heart can forgive, the heart needs to be healed. That is the healing we receive in the sacrament of Confession.

God, who created our innermost being, our spiritual heart, with the capacity to love, knows that there is nothing better for the health of the physical heart than to forgive from the heart. The double sadness in those who do not seek the healing that enables them to forgive from the heart

---

[27] Robert Enright, *Exploring Forgiveness* (The University of Wisconsin Press, 1998).

is that they continue to carry the hurt inflicted when the offence was committed, and each day they relive that hurt by ruminating on it. Those women from Northern Ireland began their exploration of forgiving with an average of seventeen symptoms indicating depression. At the end of the week these symptoms were reduced to seven. Forgiving not only heals the wounds of sin but it also lifts the spirit and infuses the joy of the Spirit.

In the sacrament of Confession we have our greatest source for the healing of the wounds of sin. As the *Catechism* says, "Healing the wounds of sin, the Holy Spirit renews us interiorly through a spiritual transformation."[28] That spiritual transformation enables us to love as Christ loves, to love even our enemies. Through the grace and presence of the Holy Spirit in the sacrament of Confession each of us, as we open our hearts and lay our inner wounds before God, receives that "life to the full" that Jesus came to give us. Hardening our hearts against those who do us wrong, by refusing to forgive, condemns us to live in resentment and bitterness, deprived of inner peace and joy.

The wounds of sin can undermine and at times almost paralyse that power to love. That is why the *Catechism of the Catholic Church* says that the confessor "leads the penitent with patience toward healing and full maturity".[29] The penitent must be led, by the light of the Spirit and

---

[28] *Catechism of the Catholic Church*, para 1695.

[29] *Catechism of the Catholic Church*, para 1466.

by the gift of discernment, to recognise the nature of the wound. Then, as the penitent opens up his or her wounded heart in the sacrament of Confession, all their sins will be forgiven and the wounds of sin will be healed. They will come away from celebrating the sacrament at peace with God, with self and with everyone in their life.

THE SACRAMENT OF THE SICK

Sickness is always a challenging time for a person. Very often as the sick person looks back on life, they can be filled with regrets. Spiritual and moral anxieties as well as physical health issues come to the fore. While the sick person needs the help of the medical doctor they also need the help of the 'physician of souls'. Our Lord Jesus Christ invites each sick person with these reassuring words: "Come to be me, all you who labour and are overburdened, and I will give you rest" (*Mt* 11:28). The rest that Christ gives is the liberation from all fear and anxiety about one's own future or about one's family, with the assurance that once we commit our past to God's mercy, all our sins are forgiven and we enter into peace of mind and heart. This coming into peace with one's whole life experience has a profound healing effect on the whole person. Herbert Benson, professor of medicine at Harvard University, was a keen observer of this effect. He wrote:

> My patients have taught me a great deal about the opportunities that emerge when artificial barriers are

broken down, about how physical ailments inspire soul-searching and a revival of meaningful living, and about how the human spirit enlivens and transforms the body.[30]

Since it is the human spirit that "enlivens and transforms the body", when the body is sick the human spirit must, as it were, work overtime, and needs support. The Church offers pastoral support in many ways, but especially through the sacrament of the Anointing of the Sick. This is how the Church introduces this sacrament:

> The Lord himself showed great concern for the bodily and spiritual welfare of the sick and commanded his followers to do likewise. This is clear from the gospels, and above all from the existence of the sacrament of anointing, which he instituted and which is made known in the Letter of James.[31]

Each Sunday, as the Gospel is proclaimed during Mass, we frequently see Jesus reaching out, touching sick people and healing them. Jesus had a very special love and concern for the sick. He knew that in their time of weakness and anxiety they needed special care and attention. He asked his disciples to have that same concern for the sick. When he sent his first disciples out to preach the gospel he gave them this commission: "Whenever you go into a town where they make you welcome, eat what is set before you.

---

[30] Herbert Benson, *Timeless Healing: The Power and Biology of Belief* (New York, 1997) p. 287.

[31] *Pastoral Care of the Sick: Rites of Anointing and Viaticum,* 5.

Heal those in it who are sick and say, the kingdom of God is very near you" (*Lk* 10:10). From the very beginning of the Church the Disciples of Christ have tried to be faithful to that commission.

In the letter of St James we read:

> If any one of you is in trouble, he should pray; if anyone is feeling happy, he should sing a psalm. If one of you is ill, he should send for the elders of the church, and they must anoint him with oil in the name of the Lord and pray over him. The prayer of faith will save the sick man and the Lord will raise him up again; and if he has committed any sins, he will be forgiven. So confess your sins to one another and pray for one another, and this will cure you (*Jm* 5:13-16).

The Apostle St James is speaking about the Sacrament of the Sick with which the Church, right from the beginning, comforted those who were sick. Today, the Church encourages us not only to ask for this sacrament, when we are sick, but also to participate in the celebration of the sacrament when a member of the family or a friend is being anointed.

A change of title

Prior to the Second Vatican Council, the Sacrament of the Sick used to be called *Extreme Unction*, the last anointing. In many people's minds it was a sign that death was imminent. Very often the priest was called to visit the sick only at the last moment. This, of course, was a great misunderstanding of the nature and purpose of the sacrament. The sacrament was seen as the "last rites" – the immediate preparation for death. Certainly, priests and others throughout the centuries have commented on the great peace and tranquillity that the sacrament brought to the seriously ill. As I wrote in an earlier book, "Sick people who were angry and bitter at their lot came to terms with dying and found acceptance and peace. Bitterness gave way to gratitude; sadness gave way to a new joy; rejection gave way to acceptance. The peaceful and holy death was seen as the fruit of the sacrament of anointing. That, of course remains the big grace. But the healing dimension of the sacrament should never be lost sight of."[32]

Sick people who are not yet in imminent danger of dying also need the grace of this sacrament. They need to come fully alive in the Spirit because, as Benson observed, "the human spirit enlivens and transforms the body." The human spirit plays a vital part in the recovery of health. As we reflect on the healing dimension of the sacrament, we will consider, in the first place, the meaning and significance of the new liturgical rite of the sacrament.

The new rite of the Sacrament of the Sick

In the Sacrament of the Sick, Christ comes in a special way to strengthen and comfort his brothers and sisters in their

---

[32] Jim McManus C.Ss.R., *The Healing Power of the Sacraments* (Redemptorist Publications, 2015) p. 96.

time of sickness and anxiety. His presence always brings peace to mind and heart. The sick person's fundamental vocation in life is to love. They now need the Lord's special grace to love everyone, and especially anyone who needs forgiveness. Sometimes it may be a member of the family who has been alienated from the family and needs the sick person's forgiveness. As we saw in the last chapter, forgiveness has great healing power. As the sick person receives the Sacrament of the Sick they receive also the grace to forgive and let go of all resentments. In the introduction to the new rite we read:

> This sacrament gives the grace of the Holy Spirit to those who are sick: by this grace the whole person is helped and saved, sustained by trust in God, and strengthened against the Evil One and against anxiety over death... A return to physical health may follow the reception of this sacrament if it will be beneficial to the sick person's salvation. If necessary, the sacrament also provides the sick person with the forgiveness of sins and the completion of Christian penance.[33]

The first gift of the sacrament is the "grace of the Holy Spirit by which the whole person is helped". The whole person is body, soul and spirit. We must always resist the materialistic view that reduces the person to the material body. We see the healing which the Holy Spirit brings as a revitalisation of the sick person's relationship with God, the source of

---

[33] *Pastoral Care of the Sick: Rites of Anointing and Viaticum*, 6.

all being. Healing means wholeness, and wholeness is the effect of spiritual well-being, not just physical well-being. It is helpful to see the difference between healing and curing.

Healing and curing

Curing is what happens in the sick organ of the body when it is restored to health; healing is what happens in the whole person, in the person's relationship with God, with others and with self. Everyone who receives and celebrates the sacrament in faith and love is certainly healed, but not everyone, with those same dispositions, is cured. Healing, in the first place, restores the sick person's relationship with God and neighbour. The vocation to love is renewed and strengthened. As the sick are led in the sacrament to lay their whole lives before the mercy of God, they come into a time of great peace. In the sacrament, all doubts, worries and fears are placed in God's hand.

The liturgy of the sacrament

The liturgy of the sacrament should be celebrated with great solemnity and, whenever possible, with the fullest participation of the sick person's family, friends and parish. It is a celebration of the word of God which calls the sick person and their friends to a renewed faith. Ideally, in his short reflection on the word of God, read during the celebration of the rite, the priest seeks to arouse this faith with a few words of encouragement.

The celebration of the sacrament includes these three prayer movements: the prayer of faith, the laying on of hands and the anointing with blessed oil. Let us consider each movement.

The prayer of faith

I remember the days when as soon as the priest walked into a sick person's room all the family and friends present left and the priest celebrated the sacrament alone with the sick person. Today the Church emphasises strongly that the sacrament is always a community celebration. In fact, the Church emphasises that the prayer of faith is said by the faithful present. In the new Rite of Anointing we read:

> The community, asking God's help for the sick, makes the prayer of faith in response to God's word and in a spirit of trust. In the rites for the sick, it is the people of God who pray in faith.[34]

The community praying the prayer of faith – that is, praying with great expectation that God will bless, comfort and heal the sick person – brings a great healing blessing on the sick person. When the sacrament is celebrated in this faith, when the sick person is led to make a complete offering of self to God, profound healing of the whole person takes place.

---

[34] *Pastoral Care of the Sick : Rites of Anointing and Viaticum, 105.*

Sickness is a time of crisis for the whole family. When serious sickness befalls a member of the family, the whole family is affected and needs to be called to greater faith and commitment. As the family members bring the sick person, with confidence, into the loving presence of God, they themselves receive God's blessing. Their faith can be strengthened and purified through the celebration of this sacrament. The priest should always pay special attention to the family so that the sickness which threatens one member will become an occasion of a new experience of trust and confidence in God for the whole family.

The laying on of hands

The laying on of hands is a very special and comforting part of the ceremony. This is how it is described in the Rite of Anointing:

> With this gesture the priest indicates that this particular person is the object of the Church's prayer of faith. The laying on of hands is clearly a sign of blessing, as we pray that by the power of God's healing grace the sick person may be restored to health or at least strengthened in time of illness. The laying on of hands is also an invocation: the Church prays for the coming of the Holy Spirit upon the sick person.[35]

Notice what we are praying for in the laying on of hands: for God's blessing on the sick person; for God's healing

---

[35] *Pastoral Care of the Sick: Rites of Anointing and Viaticum*, 106.

grace to restore the sick person to health or to strengthen them in their time of illness; for the Holy Spirit to come afresh on the sick person. This is a solemn moment in the celebration of the sacrament. Whenever it is appropriate, I invite family members to also lay their hand gently on their loved one, on the head or shoulders, or simply take a hand. This can be a moment of deep spiritual experience for the whole family, a moment of great reconciliation and forgiveness within the family. It is the opportunity to reach out in faith and love and to pray deeply for the sick member of the family. It may be the first time that the family is united deeply in prayer.

The anointing with blessed oil

Having listened to God's word, prayed the prayer of faith and laid hands in faith on the sick person, the priest is now ready to anoint the sick person with the oil blessed by the bishop during the Chrism Mass in Holy Week. As he anoints the sick person on the forehead and the palms of the hands the priest prays:

> Through this holy anointing
> may the Lord in his mercy and his love help you
> with the grace of the Holy Spirit.
> May the Lord who frees you from sin
> Save you and raise you up.

In this anointing, Christ himself, through the prayer of the priest, is asking God the Father to give the sick person the special help of the Holy Spirit. As they open their hearts to receive the Spirit of God, great healing – spiritual, psychological or physical – will take place. St Paul says, "The love of God has been poured into our hearts by the Holy Spirit who has been given to us" (*Rm* 5:5). As the sick person's fundamental vocation in life is to love, the Holy Spirit comes to enable them to joyfully live their vocation. This is the source of the peace that comes with the anointing.

After the anointing we have a choice of prayers for healing. This is my favourite one:

> Lord Jesus Christ, our Redeemer,
> by the grace of your Holy Spirit
> cure the weakness of your servant N…
> Heal his/her sickness and forgive his/her sins;
> expel all afflictions of mind and body;
> mercifully restore him/her to full health,
> and enable him/her to resume his/her former duties,
> for you are Lord for ever and ever.

This is a powerful prayer for the healing of the whole person. We pray it with expectant faith, resisting all doubts about God's plan for the sick person. Miracles do happen. Since the Church teaches that the restoration of physical health is one of the effects of this sacrament, we should earnestly request it in our prayer.

A Poor Clare's story

While I was still a young priest I received a letter from a Poor Clare Sister. During the retreat which I gave to her community she agreed to have the Sacrament of the Sick because she was suffering from acute back pain. The whole community gathered around her, laid their hands in prayer on her, and I anointed her. A few weeks later she was able to recount what had happened as a result of receiving the sacrament:

"In 1969, due to acute back pain, the specialist ordered an X-ray and it showed that a disc between two of the lumbar vertebrae was abnormally thin. This meant that when certain actions were performed, the bones rubbed together and caused pain. I was fitted with a surgical corset and I had to wear it day and night. In 1971, after a fall, I was taken to the hospital and put on traction for 14 days and fitted with another corset. Then, on Friday June 24, 1977, during our annual retreat, I received the sacrament of the sick after being prayed over for the release of the Spirit and physical healing. A few days after the retreat, when life was back to normal, I realised that my back pain was not so severe. When the days turned to weeks the pain just went, and I took the steel strips out of the corset, and then after another few weeks I left the corset off altogether and now it is collecting dust and taking up room in our cupboard! It is also a reminder to thank God for his wonderful healing power through his sacrament for the sick and also an occasion to pray for all his priests who administer his sacraments."

Because her bad back was not life-threatening she had never received the sacrament of anointing. She was surprised when I suggested that the community should celebrate the sacrament of anointing for her. She said immediately that she was happy to carry this cross that the Lord had sent her. When I asked her how she could be so sure that it was the Lord's will for her to suffer in this way, she was taken aback and said she would pray about it during the day. The next day she asked for the sacrament.

Had we not prayed for the healing, her back would not have been healed. Furthermore, had the whole community of sisters not prayed with her, as we celebrated the sacrament, I am convinced that the healing would not have taken place. It is the community that prays the prayer of faith. This experience convinced me that we should always seek to have the sick person surrounded by a believing community as we celebrate this sacrament. I realise that it is not always possible for a small community of believers to be present for the celebration of the sacrament of anointing. On this occasion all the circumstances fostered faith. These Poor Clare Sisters were a fervent community and they were making their eight-day annual retreat. During the retreat I had spoken a lot about God's healing love in the sacraments, and they believed. The sister in question was most open to the Lord and willing to do his will in all things. She would have been happy to suffer for the rest of her life because in her suffering she found union with Christ crucified. Not every sick person is physically cured but all the wounds of sin are healed.

The "gospel of suffering"

St John Paul II in his Encyclical on Suffering, written after he had been shot, speaks of the "gospel of suffering". Our society abhors suffering. We want to anaesthetise the whole world against it. We see suffering as something to be avoided at all costs. How could the Pope speak of a gospel of suffering?

Suffering in itself is not a good thing. But a good thing is concealed in suffering, namely "a particular power that draws a person interiorly close to Christ".[36] St John Paul II wrote:

> In the mystery of the Church as his Body, Christ has in a sense opened his own redemptive suffering to all human suffering. In so far as a person becomes a sharer in Christ's history – to that extent *he or she in their own way completes* the suffering through which Christ accomplished the Redemption of the world.[37]

We can speak, therefore, of "redemptive suffering". That Poor Clare Sister fully understood this. But human suffering in and by itself has no redemptive value; we fight

---

[36] St John Paul II, *Salvifici Doloris: On Suffering*, 26.

[37] St John Paul II, *Salvifici Doloris: On Suffering*, 24.

against suffering in every way we can. Human suffering, patiently accepted and lovingly united to the suffering of Christ, has a "redemptive value". Those who refuse to unite their suffering with Christ on the Cross can never recognise this value. It is a value which can be discerned only through the eyes of faith. It is a mystical value. That is why we should always pray for a renewal of faith for the sick person.

St John Paul II clearly states that suffering and death are evil, the ultimate consequence of original sin. Christ came to deliver us from this evil. In talking with Nicodemus, Jesus said, "Yes, God loved the world so much that he gave his only Son, so that everyone who believes in him may not be lost but may have eternal life" (*Jn* 3:16). The loss of eternal life would be the ultimate evil. St John Paul II said, "The only-begotten Son was given to humanity primarily to protect man against this definitive evil and against *definitive suffering*".[38]

For those who accept his salvation, Christ has destroyed the *eternal* effects of sin, namely the loss of eternal life. But the *temporal* effects of that original sin, namely suffering and death, remain in this world. St John Paul II wrote:

> Even though the victory over sin and death achieved by Christ in his Cross and Resurrection does not abolish temporal suffering from human life, nor free

---

[38] St John Paul II, *Salvifici Doloris: On Suffering*, 14.

from suffering the whole historical dimension of human existence, it nevertheless *throws a new light* upon this dimension and upon every suffering: the light of salvation.[39]

Christ enters into the world of suffering. He takes the suffering of the whole world upon himself. Because Christ is at the heart of all human suffering we can speak of a "gospel of suffering". When I said to a woman who had come through great suffering that only those who have found Christ in their suffering can really understand this kind of language, she replied, "Absolutely! But there is no other language to describe what happens to you when you really accept Christ in your sickness and suffering. It is a gospel". St John Paul II recognised this when he wrote: "Down through the centuries and generations it has been seen that in suffering there is concealed a particular power that draws a person interiorly close to Christ, a special grace."[40]

Pope Francis

In his message for World Day of the Sick, Pope Francis wrote:

The Church recognises in you, the sick, a special presence of the suffering Christ. It is true. At the side of – and indeed within – our suffering is the suffering of Christ; he bears its burden with us and he reveals its

---

[39] St John Paul II, *Salvifici Doloris: On Suffering*, 15.

[40] St John Paul II, *Salvifici Doloris: On Suffering*, 26.

meaning. When the Son of God mounted the cross, he destroyed the solitude of suffering and illuminated its darkness. We thus find ourselves before the mystery of God's love for us, which gives us hope and courage: hope, because in the plan of God's love even the night of pain yields to the light of Easter, and courage, which enables us to confront every hardship in his company, in union with him.[41]

Jesus himself prayed that God his Father would deliver him from his suffering. In his agony in the garden he prayed, "Father, if you are willing, take this cup from me. Nevertheless, let your will be done, not mine." (*Lk* 22:41). Jesus, in his own suffering, teaches us how to pray to God the Father in the times when we have to suffer pain and sickness. We pray to be relieved of the pain and suffering, we pray with faith, but, at the same time, we pray with trust in God's goodness and in his eternal plan for each of us. That is why the Church celebrates the Sacrament of the Sick with great confidence, asking for the healing of the person, a healing that is not reduced to a physical recovery, but the healing of the whole person that the Holy Spirit brings. The Second Vatican Council tells us that, "By the Anointing of the Sick priests console those who are sick."[42] It is Christ himself who is present as we celebrate the Sacrament of

---

[41] Message of Pope Francis for the Twenty-Second World Day of the Sick, 11th February 2014, 1.

[42] The Second Vatican Council, Decree on the Ministry and Life of Priests, 5.

the Sick. In the sacrament, he blesses, comforts, forgives and heals. The community of faith asks Christ with total confidence to heal the sick person in body, mind and spirit. Then we leave the final result to him. Sometimes there is a physical healing, but more frequently there is a deep, inner healing that brings the sick person into great peace.

THE EUCHARIST AND THE
HEALING OF THE WHOLE PERSON

An ancient maxim in Catholic theology says, "as the Church prays so does the Church believe".[43] If you want to find out what the Church believes about anything look at how she prays about it. When we ask what the Church really believes about God's will to heal us, we look no further than the celebration of the Eucharist, because throughout the prayers of the Mass we very frequently pray for healing. The celebration of the Eucharist is at the heart of our Christian life. As the *Catechism of the Catholic Church* says:

> The Eucharist is the 'source and summit of the Christian life'. 'The other sacraments, and indeed all ecclesiastical ministries and works of the apostolate, are bound up with the Eucharist and are orientated to it. For in the blessed Eucharist is contained the whole spiritual good of the Church, namely Christ himself, our Pasch.'[44]

---

[43] In the original Latin the maxim reads, *lex orandi, lex credendi*.

[44] *Catechism of the Catholic Church*, para 1324.

In the first section of this chapter we will look at how the Church prays for healing of body, mind and spirit, throughout the year in the celebration of the Holy Eucharist. Then, in the second part, we will look at how we participate in the celebration of Mass, which is our more familiar name for the Eucharist

Specific prayers for healing in the Eucharist

For the past fifteen hundred years, in the Roman Canon of the Mass, which was the only Canon in the Western Church until the Second Vatican Council in the 1960s, the priest has prayed:

> Remember, Lord, your servants and all gathered here, whose faith and devotion are known to you. For them, we offer you this sacrifice of praise or they offer it for themselves and all who are dear to them: for the redemption of their souls, in the hope of health and well-being, and paying their homage to you, the eternal God, living and true.

Notice the intention: "in the hope of health and well-being". Before receiving Holy Communion the priest prays silently:

> May the receiving of your Body and Blood, Lord Jesus Christ, not bring me to judgement and condemnation, but through your loving mercy be for me protection in mind and body and a healing remedy.

Just before receiving Holy Communion the priest holds up the sacred host in his hands as he proclaims, "Behold the Lamb of God, behold him who takes away the sins of the world", to which the whole assembly responds:

> Lord, I am not worthy that you should enter under my roof, but only say the word and my soul shall be healed.

The community is united in making this prayer of faith. "My soul" means my innermost self, my whole embodied self. As St John Paul II said, "The body can never be reduced to mere matter: it is a spiritualised body, just as the spirit is so closely united to the body that it can described as an embodied spirit."[45]

The prayer of faith

It is surely very significant that during the Mass the whole community cries out for health in body, mind and spirit just before they receive Our Lord in Holy Communion. The community is united in saying the prayer of faith. In the Ritual of Anointing of the Sick, as we saw in the last chapter, "The community, asking God's help for the sick, makes the prayer of faith in response to God's word and in a spirit of trust. In the rites for the sick, it is the people of God who pray in faith."[46] At Mass the people of God pray in faith and they ask for health of body, mind and spirit.

---

[45] St John Paul II, *Letter to Families* (1994), 19.

[46] *Pastoral Care of the Sick: Rites of Anointing and Viaticum*, 105.

Some post-communion prayers have very specific requests for healing. These beautiful prayers are the last prayers of the Mass and very often we don't pay close attention to them. The post-communion prayer generally consists of two parts. In the first part we thank God for the grace of the Holy Eucharist which we have just celebrated, and in the second part we ask that the grace of the Eucharist will have a specific effect in some very specific area of our life.

On the first Monday of Lent, this is how the Church gives thanks for the Eucharist and requests healing:

> "We pray, O Lord, that, in receiving your Sacrament, we may experience help in mind and body so that, kept safe in both, we may glory in the fullness of heavenly healing."

The request in this prayer is very daring. We pray to "experience help in mind and body". It is one thing to have a theoretical knowledge of God's love. It is quite another thing to experience God's healing love and to expect "to glory in the fullness of heavenly healing". To say this prayer with faith we must open our whole being to God and allow the healing love of God to fill us, removing all barriers. We open our hearts to goodness and the healing love of God and allow the presence of God's healing Spirit to renew and transform our whole being. We surrender all care and worry, all fear and doubt, and we invite God to renew us. But too often our prayer can be half-hearted. We want to be healed, but we don't want to trust; we want to be protected from anxiety, but we want to hold on to our worries; we want to forgive from the heart, but we may also want to justify ourselves and get our own back in some way.

Consider another post-communion prayer:

> We pray, O Lord God, that, as you have given these most sacred mysteries to be the safeguard of our salvation, so you may make them a healing remedy for us, both now and in time to come.[47]

Notice the word *now* in that prayer. The Church wants something to happen *now*, not tomorrow nor next week, but now! It is now, in this hour, that we need to know the healing presence of God.

Just before Christmas in 2016 this is how the Church prays for healing in the post-communion prayer:

> Lord, may participation in this divine mystery provide enduring protection for your people, so that, being subject to your glorious majesty in dedicated service, they may know abundant health in mind and body.[48]

This is a very confident prayer for abundant health. Our God is a generous God, and when we come in prayer into his presence God always wants us to ask for generous blessings.

---

[47] First Thursday of Lent.

[48] 21st December.

Finally, consider the prayer in the Mass in honour of Our Blessed Lady:

> Grant, Lord God, that we, your servants, may rejoice in unfailing health of mind and body, and, through the glorious intercession of Blessed Mary ever-Virgin, may we be set free from present sorrow and come to enjoy eternal happiness.[49]

That request for "unfailing health of mind and body", through the intercession or Our Blessed Lady, should give us great confidence as we pray for healing at Mass.

All these prayers for healing within the Mass indicate how strongly the Church believes in God's healing love, and how she expects that healing power to be experienced in the Mass.

A Catholic tradition

During the Sunday Mass, the sick members of the parish are often prayed for by name in the prayers of the faithful. The Catholic community believes that God's healing love is present and active in the Mass. Many Catholics will ask their priest to offer a Mass for the sick member of their families. They will send Mass cards to sick friends assuring them that they are being remembered at Mass. So, our Catholic faith in God's healing love in the Mass is very strong. But we have to renew our faith each time we participate in the Mass.

---

[49] Memorial Mass of Our Lady on a Saturday.

Attuning our minds to our voices

We say some wonderful prayers to God during the Mass, prayers that are asking for health in body, mind and spirit, prayers for peace in one's heart and in our communities. We have to pay attention to what we are saying; we have to mean what we say. The Second Vatican Council expressed it this way:

> In order that the liturgy may be able to produce its full results it is necessary that the faithful come to it with proper dispositions, that their minds are attuned to their voices, that they cooperate with heavenly graces lest they receive in vain.[50]

Attuning our minds to our voices is not always a simple exercise. We can be distracted, even at the most sacred moments. We are not just present at Mass, or saying our own prayers during Mass. We are participating in each part of the Mass. We try our best to participate consciously. The Second Vatican Council spoke about its hopes for our improved participation in the Mass when it stated:

> It is very much the wish of the Church that all the faithful should be led to take that full, conscious, and active part in liturgical celebrations which is demanded by the very nature of the liturgy, and to which the Christian people, "a chosen race, a royal priesthood, a holy nation,

---

[50] Constitution on the Sacred Liturgy, *Sacrosanctum Concilium*, 11.

a redeemed people" (*1 P* 2:9), have a right and to which they are bound by reason of their Baptism.[51]

Our conscious participation in the Mass

It is helpful to ask oneself this question: what are we doing during the Mass? We can identify four different actions: we listen, we respond, we offer and we receive. We will consider each action.

We listen

The first part of the Mass is called "the liturgy of the Word". The word of God is proclaimed from both the Old and the New Testaments. We try to listen very attentively because it is God who is speaking to us. As the Second Vatican Council stated very clearly:

> In the sacred books, the Father who is in heaven comes lovingly to meet his children and talks with them. And such is the force and the power of the word of God that it can serve the Church as her support and vigour, and the children of the Church as strength for their faith, food for their soul, and a pure and lasting fount of spiritual life.[52]

We try our best to listen attentively to the Readings from the Scriptures during Mass because we believe that it is God our Father who is speaking to us. Jesus says to us that

---

[51] *Sacrosanctum Concilium*, 14.

[52] Dogmatic Constitution on Divine Revelation, *Dei Verbum*, 21.

we "live by every word that comes from the mouth of God" (*Mt* 4:4). At Mass we have a special grace for filling our minds and hearts with God's word and freeing our hearts from negative and destructive words that seek to lodge in our minds.

At Mass we have a big decision to make: will we live by God's creative, life-giving word proclaimed to us in the Scripture, or will we live by a negative, destructive word that will rob us of inner peace? Living by God's word is the secret of healing in our lives. As the Psalm says. "He sent out his word and he healed them" (*Ps* 107:20). All healing comes through hearing the word of God and acting on it. As the word of God is proclaimed in the Mass we try to listen with full attention, with the hunger that the prophet Jeremiah had when he said: "When your words came, I devoured them: your word was my delight, the joy of my heart" (*Jr* 15:16).

Catholics have wonderful faith in the sacramental presence of Jesus in the consecrated bread and wine. We treat the Blessed Sacrament with profound respect. But, I believe, we struggle with Christ's presence in the word and therefore we may not listen to the word of God, proclaimed in the Scripture readings, with the same devotion with which we attend to the Consecration and the prayers of the Canon of the Mass. The real renewal of our conscious participation in the celebration of the Mass will happen when we can say with the prophet Jeremiah: "When your words came I devoured them: your word was my delight, the joy of my heart" (*Jr* 15:16).

We respond

When someone speaks to us we always respond. God speaks to us when the Holy Scriptures are proclaimed during Mass and we are invited to respond. The reader leads the congregation through a responsorial psalm inviting them to make a common response. For instance, in 2017 on the 6th Sunday of the Year, after each of four verses of Psalm 118 are proclaimed, the congregation responds: *They are happy who follow God's law.* It is very important that we try to put our heart in our responses. As we repeat the response, we deepen within our own heart the word of God that we have just heard. We cannot sincerely say, "They are happy who follow God's law" while at the same time neglecting to follow God's law through some failure to love. Our consciences will immediately alert us to this inconsistency.

We offer

After the reading of the Scriptures and the homily we then have the Offertory of the Mass. A few members of the congregation bring our gifts of bread and wine to the altar. The priest receives them and places them on the altar. What is the meaning of this action? It is our most important action during the Mass. Our full and conscious participation in the action of the Offertory is crucial.

The gifts of bread and wine have been prepared by the community and now the community are bringing these gifts so that they can be offered to God.

Symbol of the gifts

Gifts are symbols. When you give a friend a gift it is always a symbol of your love for your friend. And your friend will be grateful, not just for the material gift, the box of chocolates or the bottle of wine, but most of all for your love, which the gift represents.

Our gifts of bread and wine that we bring to the altar represent ourselves. In presenting them to God, on our behalf, the priest is offering each member of the congregation to God. Our gifts of bread and wine, like any gift we give to a friend, are a symbol of love, a sign of the love we have for God.

The gifts represent everything about us. They represent our whole being, our whole life: all the good and all the selfishness and sinfulness; all the successes and all the failures; all the joys and all the sorrows; all the hopes and all the fears. That is why I say the Offertory is our most important action during the Mass. We are offering ourselves to God. We try not to hold any area of our life back from this offering, no matter how sinful that area may seem to us. Just as your friend is grateful to receive your gift, so God is grateful to us when we sincerely give him the only gift we can, which is ourselves.

Let your Spirit come on our gifts

The priest offers our gifts of bread and wine to God and then imposes his hands over our gifts and prays:

> Make holy, therefore, these gifts, we pray, by sending down your Spirit upon them like the dewfall, so that they may become for us the Body and Blood of our Lord Jesus Christ.[53]

We are at the heart of the mystery of our faith. Over the bread and wine, on which the Spirit has come, the priest now says, in the solemn moment of the Consecration, those words of Jesus:

> Take this all of you and eat it;
> for this is my Body, which will be given up for you.

And over the wine he says:

> Take this, all of you, and drink from it, for this is the chalice of my Blood, the Blood of the new and eternal covenant, which will be poured out for you and for many for the forgiveness of sins. Do this in memory of me.

The mystery of faith

Then the priest proclaims "the mystery of faith". What has happened on the altar is not just one of the mysteries of our faith. It is the mystery which sums up in itself everything that God has done through Christ for our salvation. Christ our Saviour is truly present on the altar,

---

[53] Eucharistic Prayer II.

under the appearance of bread and wine, so that he can fulfil his promise, "He who eats my flesh and drinks my blood lives in me and I live in him" (*Jn* 6:56). We can now have the most intimate communion with the Lord Jesus as we receive him in Holy Communion, as our "bread of life", and as he answers our prayer to become "sharers in his divinity". As St John Paul II said:

> In the Eucharist we have Jesus, we have his redemptive sacrifice, we have his resurrection, we have the gift of the Holy Spirit, we have adoration, obedience and love of the Father. Were we to disregard the Eucharist, how could we overcome our own deficiency?[54]

We believe that, through the power of the Holy Spirit and the words which Jesus speaks, our gift of bread and wine becomes the Body and Blood of Christ. The sacrifice of Christ for our salvation is now sacramentally present on the altar. Jesus, "the bread come down from heaven" (*Jn* 6:58) is with us inviting us to "take and eat".

The mystery of faith is not just that bread and wine have been changed into the Body and Blood of Christ. The mystery of our faith is that the bread and wine that represent us, and everything about us, have now, through the power of the Holy Spirit, been transformed into the very Body and Blood of Christ, and we have been transformed too. We have now been made sharers in Christ's divinity. Now the priest invokes the Holy Spirit once again and prays:

---

[54] St John Paul II, Encyclical Letter *Ecclesia De Eucharistia*, 60.

Grant that we who are nourished by the Body and Blood of your Son and filled with his Holy Spirit may become one body, one spirit in Christ.[55]

This is God's will for us. We have become the Body of Christ in this world. We are no longer on our own. We are one with Christ.

Receiving and being received

We are now ready to perform the fourth action of the Mass. At Christ's invitation we come forward to receive him into our hearts in Holy Communion. This is the climax of the Mass. This is the gift that Christ came to give us. He says to us:

Anyone who does eat my flesh and drink my blood has eternal life and I will raise him up on the last day. For my flesh is real food and my blood is real drink. He who eats my flesh and drinks my blood lives in me and I live in him (*Jn* 6:54-56).

Christ is now waiting to receive us into such a complete union with himself that we become his very body in the world. As we come forward to receive Holy Communion we may sometimes forget that, in the words of St John Paul II, "*Each of us receives Christ, but also Christ receives each of us.*"[56]

This is a comforting truth because sometimes we may have been very distracted throughout the Mass and we might feel that we are badly prepared to receive Christ in

---

[55] Eucharistic Prayer III.

[56] *Ecclesia De Eucharistia*, 22.

Holy Communion. But Christ is well prepared to receive us. It was for this very moment that he came into the world so that we could become one with him. Pope Benedict XVI, speaking in Germany to a million young people, said:

> The Body and Blood of Christ are given to us so that we ourselves will be transformed in our turn. We are to become the Body of Christ, his own flesh and blood. We all eat the one bread, and this means that we ourselves become one. In this way adoration becomes union. God no longer simply stands before us as the One who is totally Other. He is within us, and we are in him. His dynamic enters into us and then seeks to spread upwards to others until it fills the world, so that his love can truly become the dominant measure of the world.[57]

We become the Eucharist we celebrate

Christ enters our hearts in Holy Communion to so transform us that we become his body in this world. In the words of Pope St Leo the Great, "Our partaking of the Body and Blood of Christ tends only to make us become what we eat".[58] The living bread that we eat in Holy Communion is not transformed into our body, rather we are transformed into Christ's body. St Augustine expressed this amazing truth:

---

[57] Homily of His Holiness Pope Benedict XVI on the occasion of the Twentieth World Youth Day, Cologne, Sunday 21st August 2005. Accessed via internet.

[58] St Leo the Great, Sermon 12 on the Passion. Cited by Raniero Cantalamessa, *The Eucharist* (Collegeville, 1995) p. 39.

He who suffered for us has entrusted to us in this Sacrament his Body and Blood, which indeed he has even made us. For we have been made his Body, and by his mercy, we are that which we receive.[59]

Our Holy Communion, therefore, is much more than receiving Christ into our hearts, wonderful though that is. It is Christ receiving us so completely into his heart that we become one Spirit with him. As we receive him we say, "Lord I am not worthy that you should enter under my roof, but only say the word and my soul shall be healed." In that solemn moment we ask for the healing that we need in body, mind and spirit. As we ask for this healing we try to dispel all doubts, all fears, and to believe in our hearts that in our union with Christ we now have all that we need for fullness of life. Christ himself says to us, "I have come that you may have life and have it to the full" (*Jn* 10:10). In our union with Christ, he will provide all that we need. Each time we receive Holy Communion we become more deeply united with Christ.

As Catholics, we love to go to Mass and receive Our Lord in Holy Communion. We become the Eucharist we celebrate.[60]

---

[59] Quoted in James T. O'Connor, *The Hidden Manna: Theology of the Eucharist* (Ignatius Press, San Francisco, 1988) p. 61.

[60] For a more detailed discussion see my book, *Going to Mass: Becoming the Eucharist We Celebrate* (Redemptorist Publications, 2015).

God the Father, in his great redeeming love, gives us Jesus his Son as the "bread of life" and, as we receive Jesus in Holy Communion, he fills us with the Holy Spirit. Holy Communion is our sanctification and transformation, because, as we eat the "bread of life" we become what we eat. We become the body of Christ. We become the Eucharist we celebrate. Now we have the great grace in Holy Communion to personally lay down all our burdens and be filled with joyful hope. As St John Paul II wrote, "The Eucharist plants a seed of living hope in our daily commitment to the work before us".[61] This living hope enables us to reach out beyond all our current troubles and embrace the future that God has in store for us. The future will be God's gift to each of us.

---

[61] *Ecclesia De Eucharistia*, 20.

FURTHER READING

Books by Fr Jim McManus C.Ss.R.

Healing in the Spirit (2002)

Inside Job: Spirituality of True Self-Esteem (2004)

The Healing Power of the Sacraments (2005)

Finding Forgiveness (Co-Author, Dr Stephanie Thornton, 2006)

All Generations Will Call Me Blessed (2007)

Hallowed Be Thy Name (2009)

Searching for Serenity (Co-Author, Dr Stephanie Thornton, 2010)

I Am My Body: Blessed John Paul's Theology of the Body (2012)

Going to Mass: Becoming the Eucharist We Celebrate (2015)

At Home in the Mysteries of Christ: The Grace of the Rosary (2016)

Embraced by Mercy (2016)

Fountain of Grace: Celebrating 150 Years of the Icon of Love (2016)

Our Spiritual Lifeline: The Oxygen of Prayer (2017)

All published by Redemptorist Publications